Wars Waged Under the Microscope

The War Against AIDS

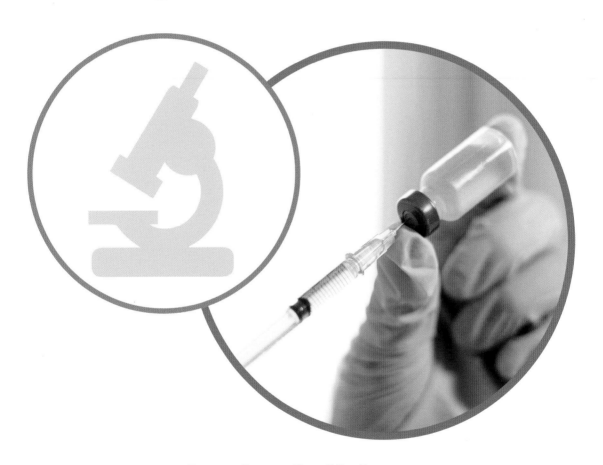

Louise Spilsbury

CRABTREE
PUBLISHING COMPANY
WWW.CRABTREEBOOKS.COM

T0014754

CRABTREE
PUBLISHING COMPANY
WWW.CRABTREEBOOKS.COM

Author: Louise Spilsbury

Editors: Sarah Eason, Jennifer Sanderson, and Ellen Rodger

Editorial director: Kathy Middleton

Design: Simon Borrough

Cover design and additional artwork: Katherine Berti

Photo research: Rachel Blount

Proofreader: Wendy Scavuzzo

Production coordinator and Prepress technician: Ken Wright

Print coordinator: Katherine Berti

Consultant: David Hawksett

Produced for Crabtree Publishing by Calcium Creative Ltd

Photo Credits

Cover: All images Shutterstock

Inside: Centers for Disease Control and Prevention: Dr. A. Harrison; Dr. P. Feorino: pp. 5; 31; Flickr: Trevor Samson/World Bank: p. 25; Shutterstock: 89stocker: pp. 23, 29; Andrey Popov: p. 21; Tewan Banditrukkanka: p. 13; Chote BKK: p. 8; Bohbeh: p. 7; Christoph Burgstedt: p 10; Choksawatdikorn: p. 16; Divasoft: p. 20; Image Point Fr: p. 22; Kim7: p. 27; B. Kuan: p. 19; Wong Yu Liang: p. 18; Monkey Business Images: p. 17; RollingCamera: p. 12; Joseph Sohm: p. 4; Take Photo: p. 14; Travel Stock: p. 26; Olena Yakobchuk: p. 11; Wellcome Collection: CC BY-NC 4.0: p. 6; CC BY 4.0: pp. 15; 28; Wikimedia Commons: Derrick Coetzee from Berkeley, CA, USA: p. 24; David Shankbone: p. 9.

Library and Archives Canada Cataloguing in Publication

Title: The war against AIDS / Louise Spilsbury.
Names: Spilsbury, Louise, author.
Description: Series statement: Wars waged under the microscope | Includes bibliographical references and index.
Identifiers: Canadiana (print) 20210189029 |
  Canadiana (ebook) 20210189037 |
  ISBN 9781427151261 (hardcover) |
  ISBN 9781427151346 (softcover) |
  ISBN 9781427151421 (HTML) |
  ISBN 9781427151506 (EPUB)
Subjects: LCSH: AIDS (Disease)—Juvenile literature. |
  LCSH: AIDS (Disease)—Treatment—Juvenile literature. |
  LCSH: AIDS (Disease)—Prevention—Juvenile literature. |
  LCSH: Epidemics—Juvenile literature.
Classification: LCC RC606.65 .S65 2022 |
  DDC j614.5/99392—dc23

Library of Congress Cataloging-in-Publication Data

Names: Spilsbury, Louise, author.
Title: The war against AIDS / Louise Spilsbury.
Description: New York, NY : Crabtree Publishing Company, [2022] | Series: Wars waged under the microscope | Includes index.
Identifiers: LCCN 2021016677 (print) |
  LCCN 2021016678 (ebook) |
  ISBN 9781427151261 (hardcover) |
  ISBN 9781427151346 (paperback) |
  ISBN 9781427151421 (ebook) |
  ISBN 9781427151506
Subjects: LCSH: AIDS (Disease)--Juvenile literature. |
  AIDS (Disease)--Treatment--Juvenile literature. |
  AIDS (Disease)--Prevention--Juvenile literature. |
  Epidemics--Juvenile literature.
Classification: LCC RC606.65 .S65 2022 (print) |
  LCC RC606.65 (ebook) | DDC 614.5/99392--dc23
LC record available at https://lccn.loc.gov/2021016677
LC ebook record available at https://lccn.loc.gov/2021016678

Crabtree Publishing Company
www.crabtreebooks.com   1-800-387-7650

Printed in the U.S.A./062021/CG20210401

Copyright © **2022 CRABTREE PUBLISHING COMPANY**. All rights reserved. No part of this publication may be reproduced, stored in a retrieval system, or be transmitted in any form or by any means, electronic, mechanical, photocopying, recording, or otherwise, without the prior written permission of Crabtree Publishing Company.

Published in Canada
Crabtree Publishing
616 Welland Ave.
St. Catharines, Ontario
L2M 5V6

Published in the United States
Crabtree Publishing
347 Fifth Ave.
Suite 1402-145
New York, NY 10016

Contents

The Enemy

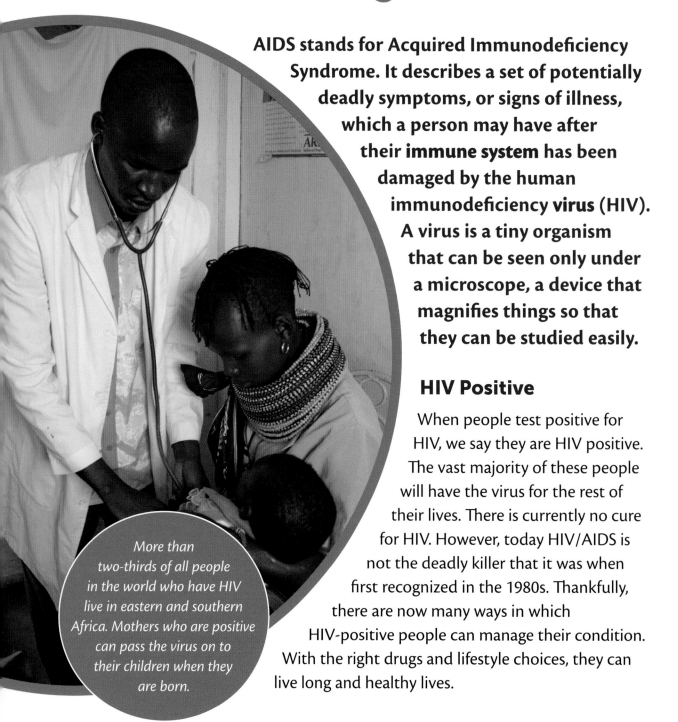

AIDS stands for Acquired Immunodeficiency Syndrome. It describes a set of potentially deadly symptoms, or signs of illness, which a person may have after their **immune system** has been damaged by the human immunodeficiency **virus** (HIV). A virus is a tiny organism that can be seen only under a microscope, a device that magnifies things so that they can be studied easily.

HIV Positive

When people test positive for HIV, we say they are HIV positive. The vast majority of these people will have the virus for the rest of their lives. There is currently no cure for HIV. However, today HIV/AIDS is not the deadly killer that it was when first recognized in the 1980s. Thankfully, there are now many ways in which HIV-positive people can manage their condition. With the right drugs and lifestyle choices, they can live long and healthy lives.

More than two-thirds of all people in the world who have HIV live in eastern and southern Africa. Mothers who are positive can pass the virus on to their children when they are born.

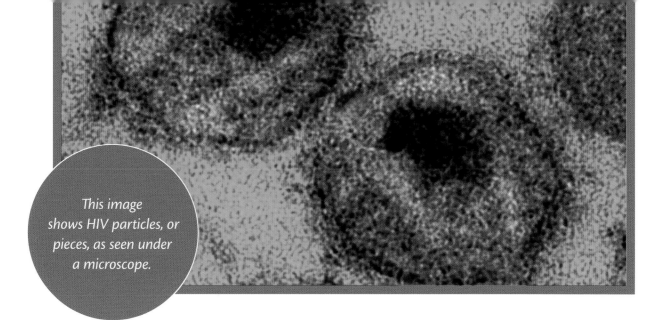

This image shows HIV particles, or pieces, as seen under a microscope.

Living with AIDS

People do not develop AIDS immediately after testing positive. This is because the virus may not attack their immune system for months or years after a positive test result. It is only when the virus begins to attack a person's immune system that they develop AIDS.

There are treatments to stop those living with HIV from developing AIDS. However, once a person with HIV has AIDS, it is highly unlikely they will recover. Usually, they die after developing different kinds of diseases, which take advantage of a weak immune system. These AIDS-related illnesses include unusual **cancers,** and a disease called tuberculosis (TB) that affects the **respiratory system**.

"

*"...being HIV positive is not a death sentence. The **eradication** of HIV/AIDS like any other disease will require a **collective** response."*

Oche Otorkpa, Researcher, School of Public Health, Texila American University

"

The Battle Begins

Scientists believe that AIDS probably began in the 1920s as a virus that affected chimpanzees in West Central Africa. They believe that the chimpanzees carried a version of an immunodeficiency virus called simian immunodeficiency virus (SIV). The virus probably crossed over to humans when people hunted and ate the animals. After SIV jumped from chimpanzees to humans, it evolved, or changed, into HIV.

A Brand-New Threat

The virus did not have a great impact on the world until 1981. Suddenly, seemingly healthy young people in the United States started dying after a mysterious disease attacked their immune systems. People were terrified of this new, frightening disease, and scientists raced to try to identify it.

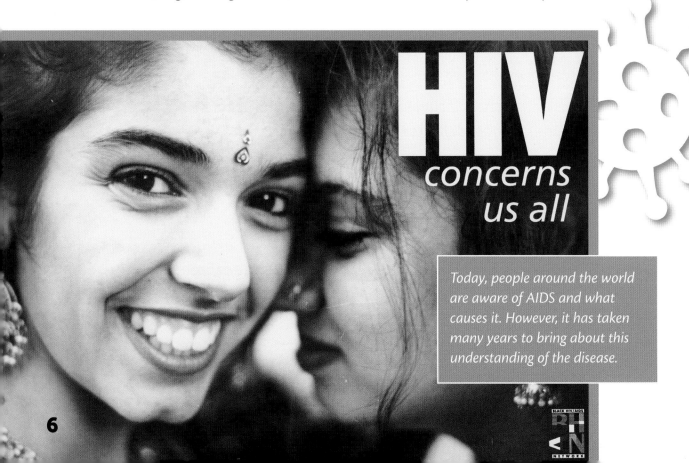

HIV
concerns us all

Today, people around the world are aware of AIDS and what causes it. However, it has taken many years to bring about this understanding of the disease.

Identifying the Enemy

Doctors studying the disease in Los Angeles and New York City discovered unusual infections in their patients. These included rare types of **pneumonia** and cancer, which were unusual to see in healthy young people. This suggested that their immune systems were not working as they should. At that time, all the patients were homosexual, or gay, men.

Naming the Enemy

Gradually, more cases of the disease were reported around the world. Then, in mid-1982, scientists realized the disease was also spreading among groups of people other than gay men, such as patients who had **blood transfusions**. They realized it was spreading through bodily fluids, such as blood and **semen**. By September that year, the disease was officially named Acquired Immunodeficiency Syndrome, or AIDS. It was not until January 1983 that the disease was also reported among the female partners of men who had AIDS.

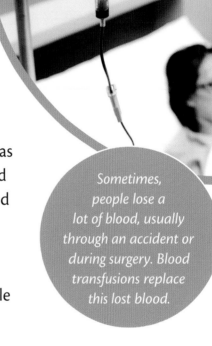

Sometimes, people lose a lot of blood, usually through an accident or during surgery. Blood transfusions replace this lost blood.

UNDER THE MICROSCOPE

Virology is the branch of science that deals with the study of viruses. In 1984, two teams of virologists, one in France and one in the United States, made a huge breakthrough when they identified the cause of AIDS: HIV. HIV was found in **samples** of **white blood cells** taken from a person who had AIDS. The scientists used special techniques to isolate, or separate, parts of the virus and a powerful **electron microscope** to identify them. This microscope can see inside the structure of viruses.

The Spread of AIDS

When doctors first started studying HIV/AIDS in 1981, all their patients were homosexual men who had unprotected sex with other men. This led to the mistaken idea that the cause of the condition was sexual, and that only gay men could get it. For that reason, the syndrome became briefly known as gay-related immune deficiency (GRID).

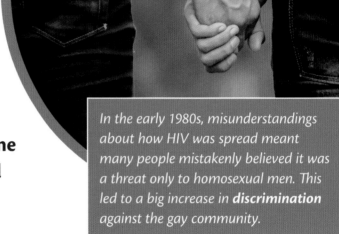

In the early 1980s, misunderstandings about how HIV was spread meant many people mistakenly believed it was a threat only to homosexual men. This led to a big increase in **discrimination** against the gay community.

The Hardest Hit

While AIDS was at first wrongly believed to be a gay-only disease, it devastated gay communities. Once it took hold in the 1980s, the disease became an **epidemic** among gay men. At first, scientists struggled to understand and deal with the mysterious new disease. They had no effective treatments for it, and as a result many gay men died. To date, the **Centers for Disease Control and Prevention (CDC)** estimates that 46 percent of all people throughout the world who have died from AIDS have been gay men. Many scientists argue that the lessons to be learned from the AIDS **pandemic** are that we must be determined in our efforts to identify and cure new diseases.

CASE STUDY: FACING THE ENEMY

The American playwright Larry Kramer was living in New York City when the disease that would become known as AIDS seemed to rapidly sicken people there. He was angry that his friends died from the disease and that governments and scientists were slow to research and find a solution to the deadly illness.

In 1982, before AIDS even had a name, Kramer set up Gay Men's Health Crisis (GMHC). This was the first group to offer support to people living with and affected by HIV. On the day the group opened a hotline, it received more than 100 calls asking for help. Then, in 1987, Kramer helped to found ACT UP, or the AIDS Coalition to Unleash Power. This group staged protests calling for research into medicines to treat HIV, and to make these drugs available more quickly and at a price everyone could afford.

Larry Kramer and other campaigners forced politicians to respond to the AIDS crisis and drug companies to treat the disease as an urgent area of research.

An Invisible Threat

While AIDS cannot be transmitted, or spread, from one person to another, HIV can. Like all viruses, HIV is invisible to the naked eye. This allows this dangerous enemy to spread unseen from person to person.

The Virus Attacks

Viruses cause damage when they get inside **cells**. HIV specifically targets cells within the human body called CD4 cells. These are a type of white blood cell in the immune system that are the body's main defenders against infection. HIV attacks and destroys these important cells, damaging the person's immune system.

Once inside a cell, the HIV virus replicates, or makes copies of itself. Those copies then quickly spread to other cells throughout the body. Next, the virus spreads to other people. Once inside their bodies, it repeats the process of replicating itself and destroying CD4 cells.

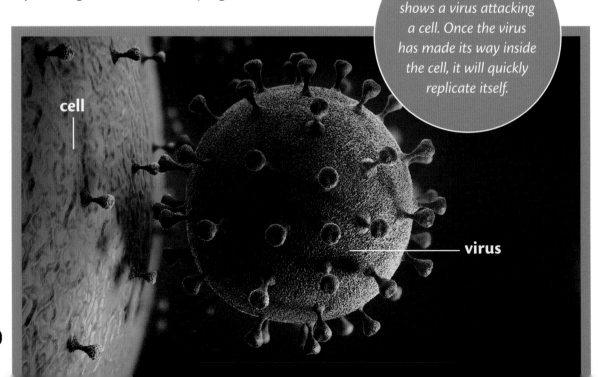

This illustration shows a virus attacking a cell. Once the virus has made its way inside the cell, it will quickly replicate itself.

cell

virus

When HIV was first discovered, people were afraid that they would get it by kissing or hugging those who were HIV positive. People today know that this is not true.

How HIV Moves

Some viruses that cause disease transmit to other people by traveling through the air. For example, when an infected person sneezes or coughs, other people inhale, or breathe in, the virus particles pumped into the air. Other viruses sit on surfaces, which people then touch and become infected. HIV is more unusual in the way that it travels.

HIV is different from most other viruses in one important way: It cannot survive outside the body for long. That means people cannot get the virus from touching someone who is HIV positive or touching the surfaces that person has touched. They can also not catch the virus by kissing and hugging a positive person. HIV is found only in certain bodily fluids such as blood and semen. It is transmitted through unprotected sexual intercourse. It can be transmitted through infected blood—for example, through cuts, when drug users share needles, and from an infected pregnant mother to the baby that she is carrying.

Under Attack

When HIV takes over a body's cells, the virus begins a slow attack of the immune system. This attack can take a long time and eventually can lead to AIDS.

HIV Infection

The first, or acute, stage of HIV/AIDS is often flu-like symptoms that appear two to four weeks after a person has been infected. These symptoms may last for a few days or several weeks. They include **fever**, chills, rash, night sweats, muscle aches, sore throat, tiredness, and mouth ulcers. These symptoms are part of the body's natural response to infection. Other infected people may not feel sick at all. Stage 2, the **chronic** stage, is when HIV is slowly reproducing and destroying CD4 cells. With medicine, this stage can be slowed and a person can stay healthy for many years. People may not have symptoms or get sick during this time.

HIV acts by gradually destroying the immune system of the infected person. The severity and timescale of the symptoms experienced will often vary from person to person. Some may experience noticeable symptoms early after infection; others may not become sick for many years.

The Onslaught of AIDS

If HIV is not treated, the viral load, or amount of HIV in the blood, will become so high it will weaken the person's immune system to the point where it cannot fight off infections as it used to. The person is then at stage 3, the most severe stage of HIV infection. They have AIDS: they will have an increasing number of severe illnesses, such as pneumonia or skin cancer. Without treatment, the patient may survive for only about three years.

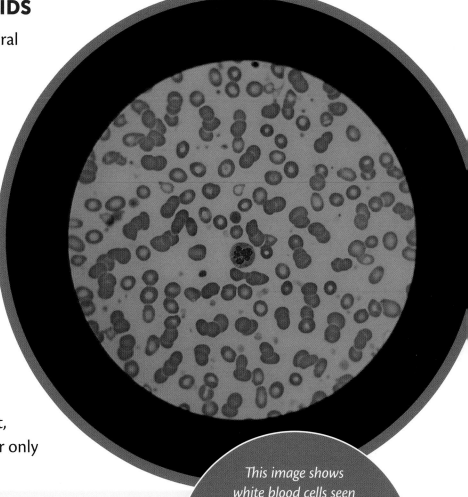

This image shows white blood cells seen under a microscope. White blood cells are part of the immune system. They can produce *antibodies*, which attack any invaders, such as viruses, that get into the body.

UNDER THE MICROSCOPE

People who have a virus such as a cold usually get better after a few days. This is because the body contains special immune cells that make substances called antibodies. The antibodies recognize and attack the virus. However, HIV is able to target these immune cells and stop them from working, so they cannot produce the antibodies needed to defeat the virus.

Studying the Enemy

Microbiology is the study of tiny organisms such as viruses. When scientists began to study HIV under an electron microscope, they could see and identify the virus by its distinctive shape and structure.

Super-Disease Virus

Researchers discovered that HIV belongs to a group of viruses called retroviruses. HIV is called a retrovirus because it works in a retro or back-to-front way. Retroviruses store their **genetic** information using a substance called **ribonucleic acid (RNA)**. To replicate when they get into a human cell retroviruses "make" **DNA** that is then added to the cell's own DNA. HIV also belongs to a group of retroviruses called lentiviruses. Lentiviruses cause disease slowly over months or years.

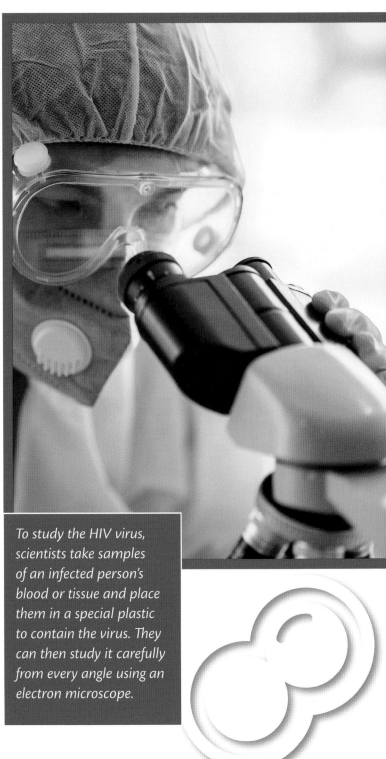

To study the HIV virus, scientists take samples of an infected person's blood or tissue and place them in a special plastic to contain the virus. They can then study it carefully from every angle using an electron microscope.

Learning How HIV Works

By studying HIV up close, scientists learned how the virus enters and uses cells. First, HIV attaches to a CD4 cell. It then joins with it and releases its genetic information into the cell. Once HIV gets inside the CD4 cell, it converts, or changes, the cell's genetic material into HIV DNA. This process is called reverse transcription. The new HIV DNA then enters the **nucleus** of the cell and takes control of it. The infected CD4 cell then produces HIV **proteins**. These are used to produce more HIV particles inside the cell. Next, the new HIV particles leave the CD4 cell, enter the person's bloodstream, and infect other cells.

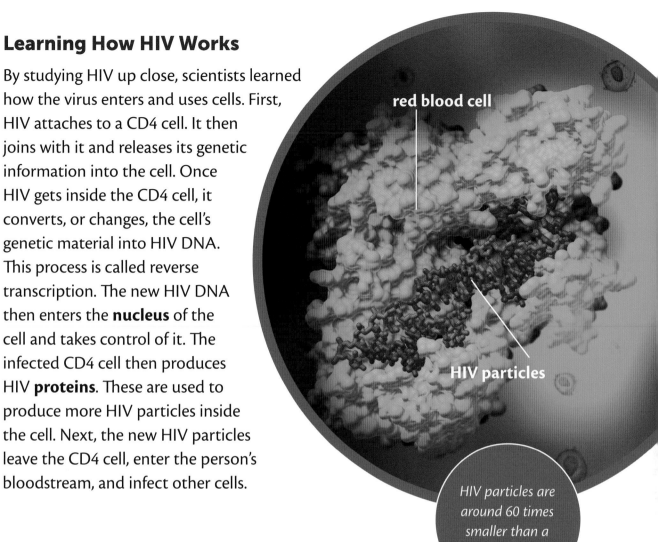

red blood cell

HIV particles

HIV particles are around 60 times smaller than a red blood cell.

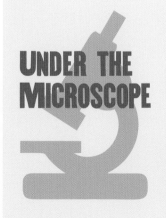

UNDER THE MICROSCOPE

HIV is a ball-shaped virus covered in spikes. The outer shell of the virus is called the envelope, and the spikes are made up of proteins called gp120 and gp41. When HIV meets a CD4 cell, the gp120 spikes lock onto the cell. The gp41 protein is used to **fuse** HIV to the cell wall. This allows the virus to enter the CD4 cell.

Weapons of War

Once scientists knew what HIV looked like, they began to develop a test to find HIV in a sample of blood taken from a patient. This first test was known as an ELISA test and it was approved for use on March 2, 1985.

Designing Weapons

The ELISA is a blood test to detect the presence of HIV antibodies in the blood. The body makes these antibodies when a person has been exposed to HIV. After the original infection, it takes about 4 to 12 weeks for HIV antibodies to appear in the blood. During this period, an HIV-positive person can still spread the disease, even though a test will not detect any antibodies in their blood. These early tests were not intended to **diagnose** patients with AIDS or HIV. Instead, they were designed to check **donated** blood for possible infection.

During the ELISA test, blood samples are placed in small tubes arranged on a plate. The plate is then placed inside the reader—a machine that scans the blood for antibodies.

CASE STUDY: SAVING LIVES

By spring 1985, 142 Americans were diagnosed with AIDS after being given blood transfusions **contaminated** by HIV. Although this was just a small section of the 9,600 people who had AIDS in the United States at that time, the nation was gripped with fear of infection through contaminated blood.

Then as now, life-saving blood transfusions were needed in hospitals and emergency treatment facilities across the United States each day. This blood is donated by millions of people. There was a pressing need to prevent these vital blood transfusions from transmitting the potentially deadly HIV. In April 1985, blood donation centers began using the ELISA test. By the end of July that same year, the nation's blood supply was declared free of HIV.

Most of the HIV tests carried out worldwide are to **screen** donated blood. This is very important in preventing the spread of HIV because the rate of transmission of the virus through infected blood is at least 95 percent.

Armed with Medicine

Once scientists understand how a virus works, they can start to look at how to weaken its effects on the body with medical treatments. They can then target and attack the enemy from within.

Drugs to the Rescue

In 1987, researchers discovered that a cancer drug used in the 1960s, which had failed to help cancer patients, stopped HIV from replicating. The medicine, known as azidothymidine (AZT), worked by blocking proteins called enzymes that the virus needs to replicate itself. The drug slowed down the virus's attack in people infected with HIV, and gave their immune systems a chance to recover and repair themselves. Drugs that slow down retroviruses, such as HIV, are known as antiretroviral (ARV) drugs.

This patient is taking his daily medicine. As with all medicines, ARVs cannot destroy viruses, but they can help people with viruses such as HIV live longer lives.

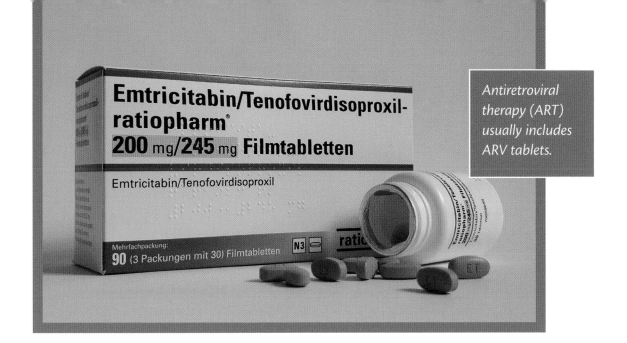

Antiretroviral therapy (ART) usually includes ARV tablets.

Working Together

As doctors began to prescribe AZT to patients with HIV, they discovered problems. The drug did not work very well on its own and it caused **side effects** such as liver problems that could be deadly. It was also very expensive. Like other viruses, HIV has the ability to evolve. It becomes **resistant** to drugs used to treat it, and they stop working. To deal with this problem, scientists developed other ART drugs, including saquinavir, which they then began to use in combination with AZT.

UNDER THE MICROSCOPE

A single ARV drug may stop most of the HIV particles in a patient from replicating, but some survive because they have a certain level of resistance. Those resistant viruses multiply, until the drug no longer works for that patient. When a patient takes several drugs together, even if a few of the viruses are resistant to one of those drugs, they will not be resistant to all of the different drugs at the same time.

Taking It to the Front Line

The goal of ART medicines is to reduce the level of HIV in the body to such low levels that blood tests cannot detect it. When a person's viral load is very low, it is said to be "undetectable" and they cannot pass on HIV to other people.

Better Testing

Better testing is an important part of getting HIV medicines to the **front line** in the war against AIDS. Early tests for HIV antibodies might only give a positive result around three months after a person became infected. The window of time when a person could spread the disease before knowing they had it was reduced to about two weeks by later HIV tests. In the 1990s and 2000s, patients began to be tested for HIV **antigens**. This helped detect the virus sooner, meaning treatment could start sooner. Today, there are several tests to monitor the health of HIV/AIDS patients.

Different tests for HIV can be performed on blood, saliva, or urine. This HIV test detects antibodies for HIV in saliva collected from a person's gums.

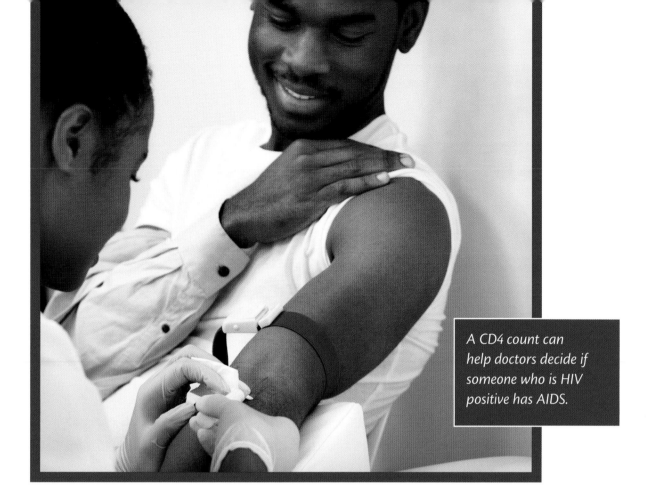

A CD4 count can help doctors decide if someone who is HIV positive has AIDS.

Counting Cells

By the mid-1990s, scientists had developed tests that measured the strength of the immune system for people with HIV and AIDS. One of these tests was called the CD4 count. It measures how many CD4 cells a person has in their blood to calculate the strength of their immune system. By 1994, CD4 counts were used to diagnose whether a person had progressed to AIDS. Now, a standard practice of HIV/AIDS testing is to have HIV-positive people do a CD4 test every six months. It helps monitor the health of their immune systems.

Finding HIV in Blood

A nucleic acid test (NAT) looks for actual HIV in the blood. First, a sample of blood is taken from a patient's vein. Then that blood is sent to a laboratory for testing. There it is examined to see if the person has HIV. The test can tell how much of the virus is present in the blood. This is known as an HIV viral-load test.

Testing New Weapons

It takes time for scientists to build new weapons against HIV and AIDS. New tests and treatments must be proven to work before they can be approved for use by governments and international organizations.

Trying It Out

All new treatments have to go through clinical trials. Clinical trials are designed to find out if a new treatment is safe, free from side effects, and better than any existing treatments. People can volunteer to take part in a clinical trial. In clinical trials, these volunteers are given a treatment that is being tested by drug companies or researchers. Volunteers agree to take part in a clinical trial because they want to help find new ways of treating health problems or because they hope the new treatment may help them.

*Patients in a **clinical trial** are monitored very carefully to see if they have any side effects. These could range from skin problems to headaches and fevers.*

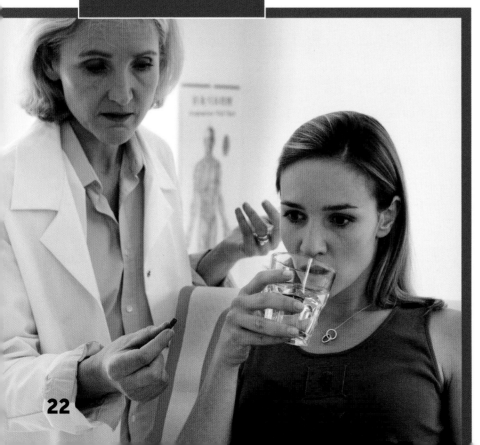

22

CASE STUDY: TRIALS BEGIN

The START clinical trial gave clear proof that an HIV-infected person should start ART medicines as soon as possible.

In March 2011, the Strategic Timing of AntiRetroviral Treatment (START) clinical trial began. The aim of the trial was to test whether starting to take ART medicines earlier would help people who were HIV positive.

Before this trial, people with HIV were told to wait until their CD4 count was low before they started taking ART medicines. The START clinical trial was carried out at 215 sites in 35 countries and involved 4,685 men and women with HIV, aged 18 and older, who had never taken ART. Half of the volunteers were chosen at **random** to start ART immediately. The other half did not start treatment until their CD4 cell count declined to below a certain level. The results were astonishingly clear. The half of the trial that started immediately showed a huge reduction in serious illness and death. This clearly proved that taking the right drugs sooner rather than later could help save millions of lives.

New Weapons

Scientists are working hard to create a vaccine for HIV/AIDS. To do so, they must use their knowledge of the virus by examining it under microscopes to try to create a method that will disarm it.

The Ultimate Weapon

Vaccines are substances given when a person is healthy to teach their immune system to detect and defend against harmful viruses. They encourage a stronger immune reaction in the body. That way, the person will not become sick if the viruses enter their body later. There are hopes that current scientific tests of a vaccine will soon be completed in parts of Africa. This would be a huge breakthrough.

Education and early testing is vital in the ongoing fight against HIV/AIDS. This truck in Berkeley, California, is offering free HIV tests and information to people in the area.

The Hope for a Cure

Scientists are also working on finding a cure for HIV. In 2007, Timothy Ray Brown was given a **bone marrow** transplant to treat the blood cancer he had developed because he was HIV positive. The transplant came from a **donor** who had a rare mutation, or change in form, in their DNA that is resistant to HIV. Incredibly, the treatment cured Brown of HIV. Brown died in September 2020 after his cancer returned. In 2020, Adam Castillejo was cured using a similar treatment. Unfortunately, such treatment is too risky and aggressive to use on every HIV patient, but it does give hope that one day a cure will be found.

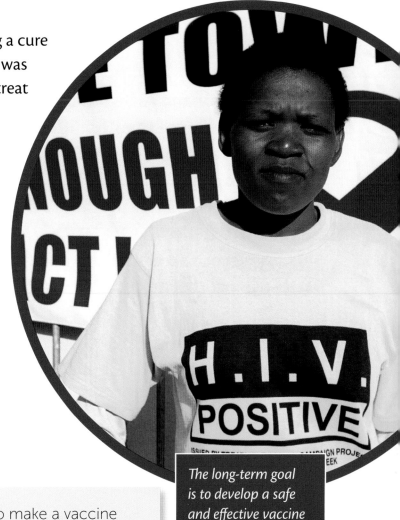

The long-term goal is to develop a safe and effective vaccine that protects people worldwide from acquiring HIV.

UNDER THE MICROSCOPE

It's difficult to make a vaccine for AIDS because the HIV virus is so complicated. The virus also changes over time, so just one strain, or type, of vaccine may not work. A team of international researchers is testing a new type of vaccine that is made from many different virus strains rather than from one single type. The idea is that it will encourage immune responses that can tackle all forms of HIV/AIDS.

Future Warfare

The war on HIV and AIDS has been long, but largely successful. There are now more than 30 different HIV medicines available, and early treatment using ARTs can stop HIV-positive people from developing AIDS. Drugs can also stop transmission at birth from a positive mother to her child. With the right treatment, people who are HIV positive can live normal lives. However, there is still no cure for AIDS, so the battle against this devastating disease continues.

Keeping Up the Effort

Between 2000 and 2019, new HIV infections fell by 39 percent, and HIV-related deaths fell by 51 percent. However, because testing and drugs are expensive, many people cannot afford them and so the disease has continued to spread. Around 690,000 people died from HIV-related causes in 2019, and 1.7 million people were newly infected. Ninety percent of children with HIV live in sub-Saharan Africa. To close this gap in treatment, affordable prices are being negotiated for ARVs. Improved ways of getting tests and medicines to people are being found.

AIDS has made many children *orphans*. These children are at a school in Eswatini in southern Africa. Ten percent of the children in that country have become orphans because their parents have died from AIDS.

Reducing Risk

Experts believe that HIV vaccines and cures will become a reality in the future. In the meantime, HIV and AIDS education programs are important in encouraging prevention. Prevention includes abstaining from, or not having, sex and using a **condom** for all types of sex. It also includes getting regular testing for HIV, and using **sterile** injection equipment (including needles and syringes) for each injection of drugs and medicines. World AIDS Day, which takes place on December 1 each year, reminds people there is still a vital need to raise money, increase awareness, fight prejudice, and improve education about HIV/AIDS.

On World AIDS Day, people wear a red ribbon to show they support the fight against HIV, the people living with HIV, and to remember those who have died from an AIDS-related illness.

"*Three decades into this crisis, let us set our sights on achieving the 'three zeros'— zero new HIV infections, zero discrimination, and zero AIDS-related deaths.*"

Ban Ki-Moon, Secretary-General, United Nations (UN)

Timeline

Track HIV/AIDS from its first appearance through to breakthrough treatments.

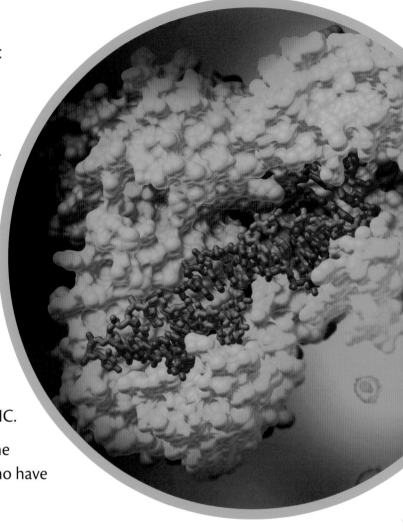

1981   Cases of cancers and other serious diseases start spreading among young and otherwise healthy gay men in New York and California.

1982   The Centers for Disease Control (CDC) uses the term "AIDS" for the first time.

1982   Larry Kramer sets up GMHC.

1983   AIDS is reported among the female partners of men who have the disease.

1984   The HIV virus is identified.

1985   The ELISA test to find HIV in blood is approved for use.

1985   By the end of July, the blood supply in the United States is declared free of AIDS after ELISA testing.

1987   Larry Kramer helps found ACT UP, a protest group calling for research into HIV medicines.

1987   The first medicine to prevent HIV from replicating, called AZT, is tested.

1994   A CD4 count becomes the standard way to diagnose a person with AIDS.

1995   An alternative HIV drug called saquinavir is developed.

2007   Timothy Ray Brown is cured of HIV after a bone marrow transplant.

2011   The START clinical trial proves that an HIV-infected person should start ART urgently.

2019   Approximately 38 million people are still living with HIV/AIDS.

2020   Adam Castillejo is cured of HIV using a similar treatment to Brown in 2007.

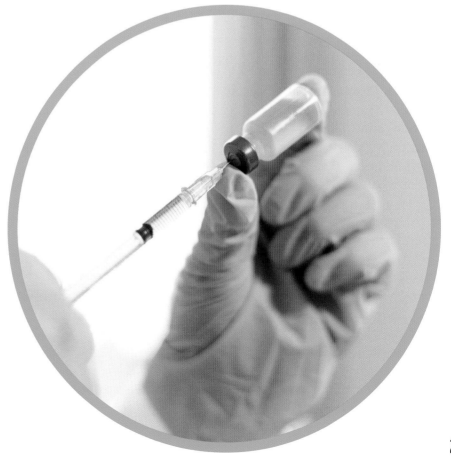

Glossary

antibodies Substances that the body produces to fight disease

antigens Invaders in the body, such as viruses

blood transfusions Giving donated blood

bone marrow Spongy tissue inside some bones that contains stem cells. These develop into different types of cells, including white blood cells that fight infections.

cancers Diseases caused by an uncontrolled division of abnormal cells in a part of the body

cells The smallest units of a living thing that can survive on their own, carrying out a range of life processes

Centers for Disease Control and Prevention (CDC) An American organization using scientific research to find ways to protect the public's health

chronic Serious and lasting for a long time

clinical trial Research performed on people to discover more about disease treatments

collective Done as a group

condom A barrier device used during sexual intercourse to reduce the chances of pregnancy or transmitted infections

contaminated Infected

diagnose To confirm a person has an illness

discrimination The unfair treatment of people based on factors such as their race, gender, age, or sexual orientation

DNA Deoxyribonucleic acid—a part of the body's cells that gives each individual their own unique characteristics

donated Given by another person

donor A person who gives something

electron microscope A high-powered microscope that uses beams of electrons instead of rays of light

epidemic When a large number of people within one community or country have a particular disease

eradication Complete removal

fever A high body temperature

front line An area of greatest danger

fuse To become one

genetic Relating to genes, which carry instructions for how the body works

immune system The body organs and cells that produce substances to help it fight infections and disease

nucleus The control center of a cell

orphans Children whose parents have died

pandemic When a large number of people across the world have a particular disease

pneumonia An infection that inflames the air sacs in one or both lungs

proteins Substances that do most of the work in cells

random In no particular order

resistant Able to withstand things that might affect it

respiratory system The organs that allow a person to breathe

ribonucleic acid (RNA) A substance found in viruses and cells that contains genetic information

samples Small amounts of something, such as blood, for testing

screen To test or examine something

semen The bodily fluid containing sperm

side effects Unwanted symptoms caused by medical treatment

sterile Totally clean and free from bacteria or viruses

vaccine A substance that helps protect against certain diseases

virus An infectious microscopic living thing that can cause sickness and only replicates in living organisms

white blood cells Cells that attack and destroy enemy invaders, such as viruses

Learning More

Find out more about HIV/AIDS and how the war against this deadly disease is being won.

Books

Dakers, Diane. *Magic Johnson: Basketball Legend, Entrepreneur, and HIV/AIDS Activist* (Crabtree Groundbreaker Biographies). Crabtree Publishing Company, 2016.

Simons, Rae. *A Kid's Guide to AIDS and HIV* (Understanding Disease and Wellness: Kids' Guides to Why People Get Sick and How They Can Stay Well). Village Earth Press, 2016.

Thompson, Elissa and Paula Johanson. *Coping with HIV and AIDS*. Rosen Young Adult, 2019.

Whitehead-Brice, Miriam. *My Grandma is HIV Positive*. Imagination Press LLC, 2019.

Websites

Learn more about HIV and AIDS at:
https://kidshealth.org/en/kids/hiv.html

Read the facts about HIV in Africa at:
www.dosomething.org/us/facts/11-facts-about-hiv-africa

Get more information and in-depth facts at:
www.who.int/health-topics/hiv-aids/#tab=tab_1

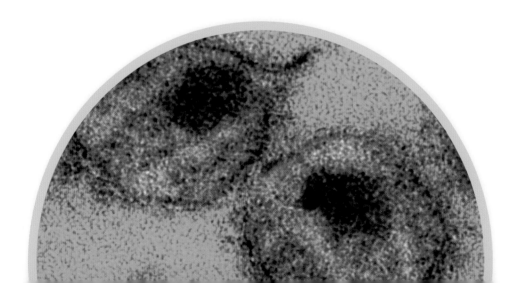

Index

A B O U T   T H E   A U T H O R

Award-winning author Louise Spilsbury, who also writes under the name Louise Kay Stewart, has written more than 250 books for young people on a wide range of subjects. When not tapping away at her computer keys, she loves swimming in the sea and making bonfires on the beach near her home.